You Can Draw Animals

Right Down to the Skin!

BY JIM BRADRICK

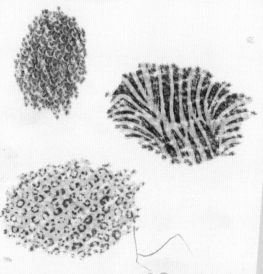

tangerine Press®

becker&mayer! BOOKS

SPECIAL THANKS TO LILA BECKER AND ASHLEY STEINMETZ FOR PRODUCT TESTING.

W9-AHL-448

INTRODUCTION

The twelve animals in this book show the great variety of patterns and textures in the animal kingdom. Most animals have scales, feathers or fur. Some have unique patterns everyone recognizes, like zebra stripes or leopard spots. Other patterns and textures are shared by many animals, like the fur of a bear.

The pictures in this book are simplified to make them easy for you to draw and to show off the textures you will rub on at the end. Each exercise in this book includes everything you need to draw the animals. If you follow the directions carefully, everybody you show your pictures to will know what they are! The step-by-step directions show you how to draw the animals. Then you rub on the textures—that's the best part!

Drawing has always been important to me. I have spent most of my life learning how to draw better. I went to art school for two years, where I learned about color, painting, and figure drawing. I taught myself cartooning and animation, and I have drawn for comic books, advertising cartoons, and animated television commercials. Animation is my favorite form of drawing, because the drawings come to life!

And you know what? I am still learning! If you want to become an expert at anything, you must practice a lot.

I hope you will have as much fun using this book as I had in making it for you.

Jim Bradrick

JIM BRADRICK, ARTIST & AUTHOR

JIM BRADRICK IS AN ARTIST AND ANIMATOR WHO CREATES AWARD-WINNING CHILDREN'S SOFTWARE. JIM LIVES WITH HIS WIFE, JONI, IN WOODINVILLE, WASHINGTON.

CREATURE COVERINGS

Animals are covered with scales, feathers or fur. Their coverings help them survive in the wild.

SCALES help reptiles hold onto moisture, to keep their skin from drying out under the hot sun.

FEATHERS keep birds warm and dry and help them fly.

FUR helps mammals keep warm. Many have thicker coats in winter, then shed the fur to keep cool in summer. A lighter coat helps protect them from the sun's rays.

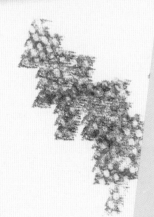

CAMOUFLAGE patterns on animals' coats help them hide from predators or stalk their prey. Stripes or spots help animals hide in the shadows made by grass, rocks, or trees. Certain patterns or colors help some animals blend in, because their coats match the grass, sand, snow, or water. This makes it hard for other animals to see them.

RUBBING INSTRUCTIONS

MAKE YOUR OWN ANIMAL "RUBBING" DRAWING

TORTOISE

HOW TO USE THE TEXTURES IN THIS BOOK

1. Remove the plastic sheet from the back of the book.

2. There are twelve different texture tiles on it — six on each side. (If you can't tell which is which, they have labels underneath them!)

3. Choose one (or more!) of the skin, fur and feather texture tiles from the plastic sheet. Set the plastic sheet aside until you have made your line drawing.

4. Decide if your drawing will be in color or in black and white.

5. Set aside pencils, crayons, chalk, paper — everything you'll need for your picture.

6. Look over the animal drawing you want to make. Read the four steps. Follow the directions to make your own animal!

ZEBRA

ARMADILLO

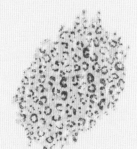
LEOPARD

7. When you are done, look it over. Do all of the lines connect? (There should not be any broken lines, because what you are making is a "line drawing" of that animal.)

8. Do the eyes seem to be looking at something? Maybe you can draw that in your picture too! Where does your animal live? Add trees, water, sky – anything else you want in your picture.

9. Now, carefully place your drawing over the texture tile. Slide it around until your animal drawing is right on top of the texture.

10. Lightly color over the texture tile until – presto! – you see the pattern! Your pencil or crayon works best if you hold it sideways, instead of pressing on the pencil point.

11. You will probably have to move your drawings across the tile so that you can fill in all the areas of the body.

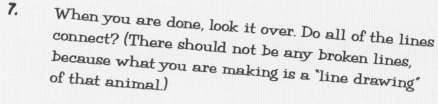

ELEPHANT

FISH

ALLIGATOR

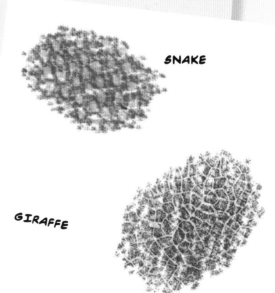

SNAKE

GIRAFFE

(THERE'S MORE!)

EAGLE

MORE RUBBING INSTRUCTIONS

- See how some areas on the texture tiles have special sections? The tortoise texture tile has an area just for the tortoise's legs. (You can find this on the lower part of the tortoise texture tile.) The texture tile for the eagle has a special area for the feet too –can you find it?

DINOSAUR

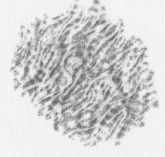

- For a darker pattern, press down a little more. Or, color over it again and again. (Warning! Do not press too hard! You could make a hole in the paper.)

- Make sure your strokes are not too long, or too wide. If you go outside the lines of your animal drawing, you will have spots, fur or feathers outside of your animal!

- Put the finishing touches on your picture. Show it off to your family and friends!

BEAR

Go WILD!

IF YOU MAKE YOUR DRAWINGS REALLY SMALL, YOU CAN MAKE ANIMALS WITH REALLY BIG SCALES!

CREATE YOUR OWN COLORS

Make the line drawing of your animal one color, then rub over it with another color. Experiment with primary colors, like yellow over blue, to make the shade you want. (For example, yellow and blue make green.)

PICK CRAZY COLORS FOR YOUR RUBBING!

Ask your family or friends, "Ever see an orange armadillo... or a purple alligator?"

HOWDY!

ADD WORDS TO YOUR PICTURE... MAKE YOUR OWN PICTURE BOOK!

What happens when your elephant meets your giraffe?

MIX-AND-MATCH PATTERNS

Ever see a leopard with zebra stripes? How about a fish with a furry head and a feathery tail?

Draw more than one animal in your picture, to make a whole scene. You might have an eagle flying in the sky, while an alligator crawls in the mud below. Or, you might draw a bear stalking a fish.

EXPERIMENT!

Try different things! Color the whole animal, then use an eraser over the texture to see the pattern. (It looks like a photo negative.)

USE YOUR IMAGINATION!

7

MAKE AN ARC ON EACH
SIDE OF A LINE

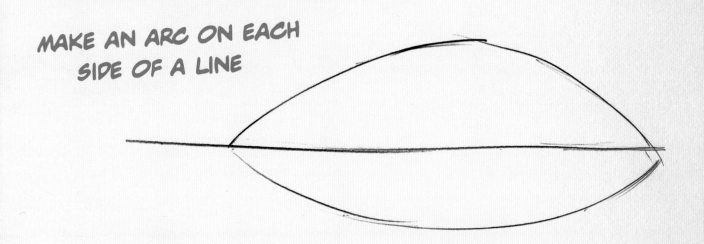

SKETCH IN
THE FINS
AND TAIL

AND THE GILL

MAKE THE
ENDS OF THE FINS
MORE CURVED

PUT THE EYE AND
MOUTH IN
THE RIGHT
PLACE

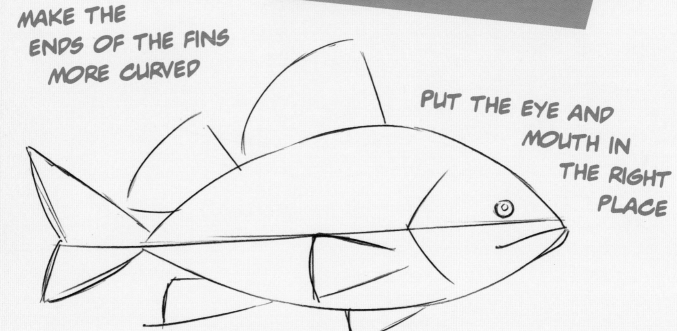

NOW ERASE
THE LINES YOU
DON'T NEED

AND ADD
THE DETAILS!

FOR THE SNAKE, FIRST DRAW
THE BRANCH IT WILL HANG ON

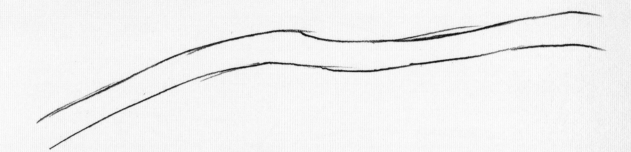

THINK OF THE SNAKE'S BODY
AS A GARDEN HOSE...

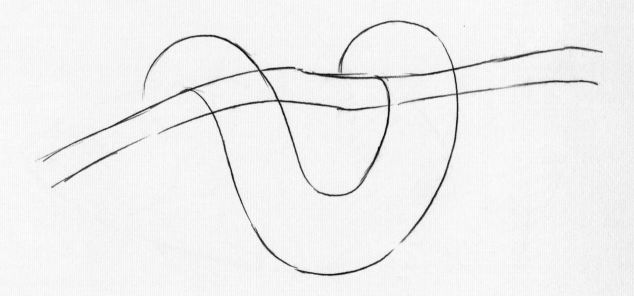

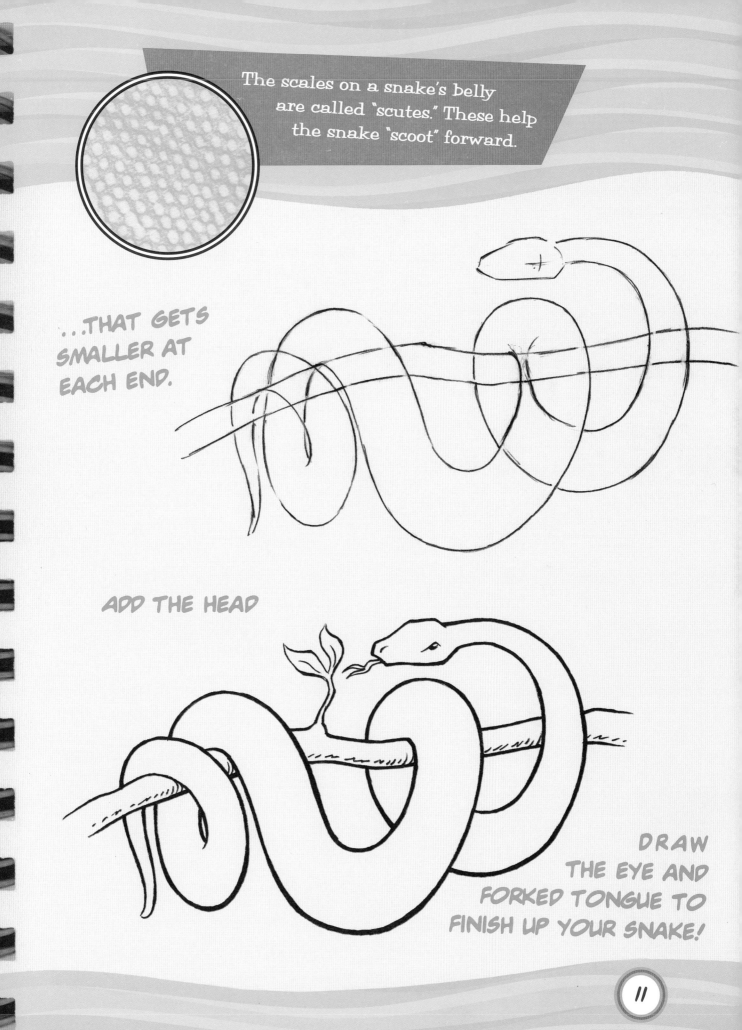

The scales on a snake's belly are called "scutes." These help the snake "scoot" forward.

...THAT GETS SMALLER AT EACH END.

ADD THE HEAD

DRAW THE EYE AND FORKED TONGUE TO FINISH UP YOUR SNAKE!

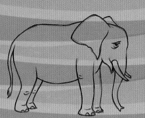

Elephant

AN OVAL
FOR THE HEAD,
AND A BIGGER
ONE FOR
THE BODY

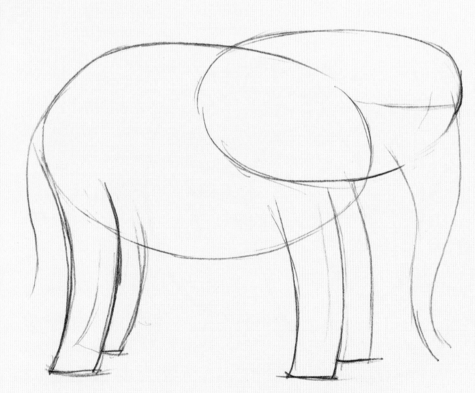

ADD
THE LEGS
AND TRUNK

Elephants' skin is so thin, they get sunburned! They cover themselves with mud to block out the sun's rays.

WITH THE EARS, EYE AND TUSKS DRAWN, IT REALLY LOOKS LIKE AN ELEPHANT!

NOW CLEAN IT UP AND IT'S READY FOR THE CIRCUS!

HOW TO DRAW AN Armadillo

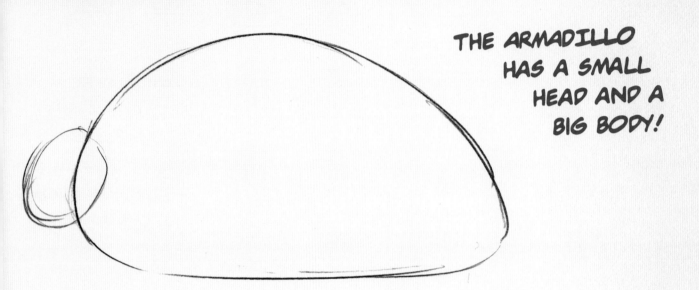

THE ARMADILLO
HAS A SMALL
HEAD AND A
BIG BODY!

ADD THE NOSE
AND FEET

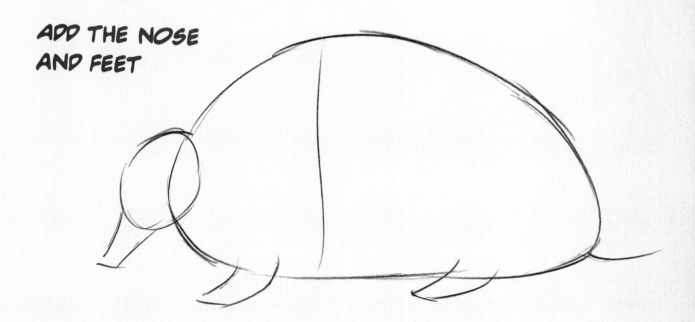

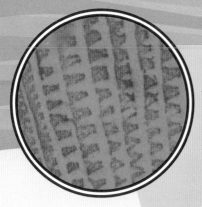

An armadillo's scaly coverings are made of flexible bones. The plates are separated by skin and even a few white hairs.

ADD THE EARS AND EYE

AND YOUR LITTLE ARMADILLO IS DONE!

FOR THE
TORTOISE,
START
WITH THE
SHELL

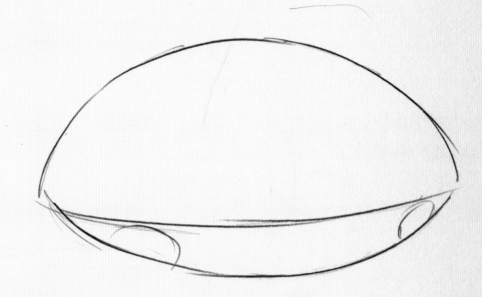

PUT IN THE LEGS,
NECK, AND HEAD

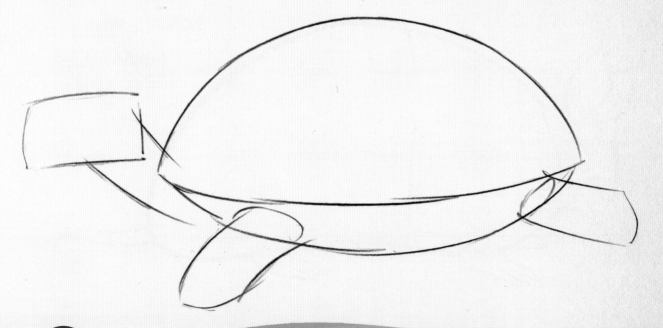

First a tortoise pulls its head into its shell, then its front legs. Inside, the head fits in-between the front legs. In front of the head, the front feet are touching. Its back feet block the "holes" at the back of its shell.

MAKE
THE NECK
"WRINKLY"

AND MAKE
HIS MOUTH
A SHARP
BEAK!

START WITH
TWO OVALS,
BIG AND
SMALL

ADD A
ROUND HEAD FOR THE BEAR

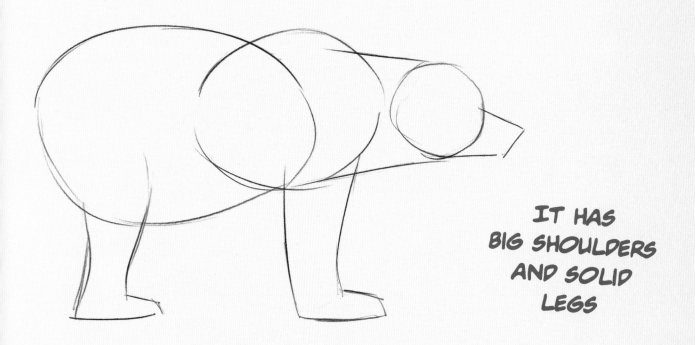

IT HAS
BIG SHOULDERS
AND SOLID
LEGS

A polar bear uses solar energy to stay warm. Even though it looks white, a polar bear's hair is really transparent ("see-through"). So sunlight gets through and is absorbed by the bear's black skin. Then the fur traps the sun's heat close to the skin (to keep warmth in and cold out).

IT HAS ROUND EARS AND A SHORT TAIL!

YOUR BEAR IS FINISHED!

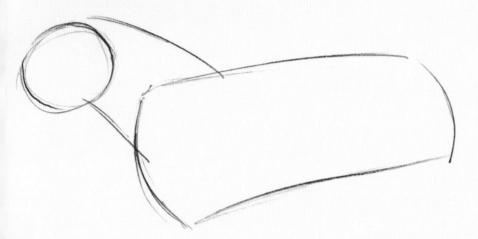

START WITH THESE SIMPLE SHAPES

ADD THE LEGS, NOSE AND EARS

A leopard has a thick undercoating of fur on its belly to protect it from the kicks of its prey.

DRAW THE EYE AND CURVE OF THE TAIL

AND IT'S READY FOR SPOTS!

A ZEBRA IS A MEMBER OF THE HORSE FAMILY

SEE HOW THE FRONT LEG IS DIFFERENT FROM THE BACK?

A zebra's skin is black and its hair is white.

ADD THE OTHER TWO LEGS, HIS MANE AND EARS!

A ZEBRA'S MANE IS STIFF, LIKE A BRUSH!

NOW IT NEEDS STRIPES!

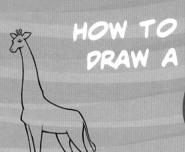
FOR A GIRAFFE,
START WITH THE LONG NECK
AND SLOPING BACK

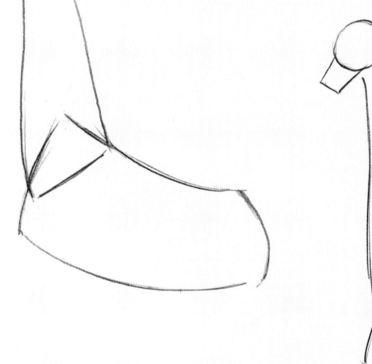

ADD LONG LEGS AND
A SMALL HEAD TO MAKE
IT LOOK LIKE A GIRAFFE --
ALREADY!

ADD THE FEATURES OF THE HEAD

Each giraffe has its own pattern on its coat. Like human fingerprints, no two giraffes have the same pattern of spots.

AND THE OTHER LEGS!

NOW YOUR GIRAFFE IS FINISHED!

THIS LOOKS LIKE
AN ALLIGATOR ALREADY!

NOW ADD THE
LEGS AND FEET

Baby alligators do not look like their parents. Their skin has bright stripes and yellow blotches. As they grow, the stripes and blotches fade as the alligators become a darker color.

THEN THE EYES AND MOUTH

WITH A FEW MORE DETAILS, HERE'S YOUR ALLIGATOR!

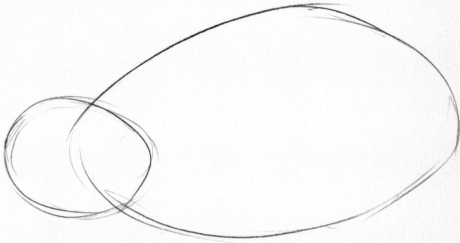

START OUT
LIKE YOU DID
FOR THE
ELEPHANT

ADD A BEAK,
LIKE YOU DID
FOR THE
TORTOISE

Fossils have given us clues as to what dinosaur skins might have looked like. They are impressions made by scales, feathers or fur.

DRAW THREE BIG HORNS!

IT'S A TRICERATOPS!

YOU CAN START YOUR SOARING EAGLE WITH TWO LINES -- ONE ACROSS THE WING, OR ONE THROUGH THE BODY

OR YOU CAN START WITH THE SHAPES OF THE HEAD, BODY, AND TAIL

AND THEN ADD THE TWO LINES

30

Baby bald eagles do not look like their black-and-white-feathered parents. They are brown until they lose these feathers and grow black and white ones.

ONCE YOU'VE PUT THEM ALL TOGETHER, ADD THE BEAK AND THE FEET

AND YOUR EAGLE IS FLYING!

 1 FISH

2 SNAKE

3 ELEPHANT

4 ARMADILLO

 5 TORTOISE

6 BEAR

 7 LEOPARD

 8 ZEBRA

 9 GIRAFFE

 10 ALLIGATOR

 11 DINOSAUR

 12 EAGLE

becker&mayer!
BOOKS

Copyright © 2002 by becker&mayer!, Ltd.
Published by Tangerine Press, an imprint of Scholastic Inc.,
557 Broadway, New York, NY 10012.
All rights reserved.

Tangerine Press®

If you have questions or comments about this product,
send e-mail to infobm@beckermayer.com.

Written and Illustrated by Jim Bradrick
Product Design by Chris Tanner
Art Direction by J. Max Steinmetz
Graphic Design by Amy Redmond
Edited by Susan Jankowski
Project Management by Beth Lenz
Graphic Production by Sabine Asher

10 9 8 7 6 5 4 3 2
04258
ISBN 0-439-42467-4

Printed, manufactured, and assembled in China.